DESPERATELY SEEKING BASQUIAT

IAN CASTELLO-CORTES

GINGKO PRESS

A VERY BRIEF CHILDHOOD

By most measures, Jean-Michel Basquiat, had a confused and somewhat traumatic childhood. Born in 1960 to a Haitian father and Puerto Rican mother, he went to predominantly white schools at a time when racism in New York was rife. His upbringing was bourgeois, a home seemingly safe on the surface. But Matilde, Basquiat's mother who first encouraged and nurtured her boy's interest in art, suffered from serious mental illness and was in and out of institutions. When Basquiat was seven, his parent's tempestuous marriage ended in separation. Henceforth, Basquiat was brought up by his disciplinarian father. He had to grow up young and ran away from home aged 15. But he discovered gang and graffiti culture on the street and, before he was 17, had garnered attention from *The Village Voice* amongst others, with his and his friend Al Diaz's invention of their graffiti SAMO© taglines.

"SAMO© AS A CONGLOMERATE
OF DORMANT GENIUS"

"MY MOUTH / THEREFORE AN
ERROR"

"SAMO©...4 THE SO-CALLED AVANT
GARDE"

"SAMO©...AS AN END TO THE
9 TO 5 "I WENT TO COLLEGE"
"NOT 2-NITE HONEY"

"SAMO©...AS AN ALTERNATIVE 2
'PLAYING ART' WITH THE 'RADICAL
CHIC' SECTION OF DADDY'S FUNDS..."

"SAMO©...AS AN ALTERNATIVE TO
GOD'

①

PARK SLOPE

"We come from an elite, affluent background in Haiti."
Gérard Basquiat

Like quite a few ground-breaking, uber cool artists, Basquiat's background was safe, moderately aspirational, one might even say suburban and conventional. His father, Gérard, an accountant, considered himself to be smart, a cut above, and the neighbourhood he and his wife Matilde chose to initially settle in, was certainly not the ghetto, but one of comfortable brownstones close to Brooklyn Park. At the time that Basquiat was born, Park Slope had an eclectic population of whites, hispanics and blacks, mostly professional, upwardly mobile and ambitious. It was the early sixties, and the US economy was on the up in that pre-Vietnam wave of American optimism. Gérard, from a well-established bourgeois family, had been obliged to leave Haiti due to the political situation. He carried an innate sense of self-worth from his previous status in Haiti with him to New York.

WHERE?
ROW OF BROWNSTONES,
PARK SLOPE,
BROOKLYN,
NEW YORK.

2

BASQUIAT SENIOR

"I was under tremendous pressure as a single parent. I was a strict parent, but not a severe one." **Gérard Basquiat**

Basquiat senior was tough, ambitious for himself and his children, with the grit to put himself through night school to get his accountancy qualifications. These landed him a job at the prestigious publishers Macmillan. To his neighbours he appeared highly sophisticated, always smartly turned out, a member too of the local tennis club. Much has been made of the trauma that Basquiat suffered as a result of his father's strict and physical disciplining of a son he did not fully understand. It's hard to measure what goes on in a family home, but in this Gérard was probably not acting outside the norms for his background and time; 1950s and '60s parenting was not enlightened. Few children were listened to and thrashing out any resistance, when the chips were down, to parental authority was pretty standard. The children who suffered most were those who were wilful or overly sensitive. Basquiat happened to be both.

WHO?
GÉRARD BASQUIAT.

③

FLATBUSH

"Basquiat's mother was in and out of mental hospitals." Andy Warhol, *Diaries*

When Basquiat was five, the family moved to Flatbush, a slightly less salubrious neighbourhood in Brooklyn. Under the respectable surface, there were huge tensions. According to Basquiat his Puerto-Rican mother, Matilde Andrades, suffered from severe depression and bouts of violence towards Gérard as well as her son. She and Gérard had the trauma of losing their first child, Max, aged just one. Unlike her husband, she was the one with the artistic temperament and Basquiat credits her for encouraging his early ability in drawing: "the art came from her" he later said. Cultured, and speaking English, French and Spanish, she recognised his obsession with drawing and encouraged his interest, taking him to the Brooklyn Museum, MoMA and the Met. Basquiat rarely discussed Gérard and Matilde's divorce, when Basquiat was seven years old. But the loss of stability and of his main creative inspiration must have been traumatic.

WHERE?
JUNIOR'S RESTAURANT,
FLATBUSH AVENUE,
BROOKLYN.

④

GRAY'S ANATOMY

"Was Jean-Michel unhappy because I left his mother? I don't know. I mean who knows what goes on in the minds of children?"
Gérard Basquiat

Just as the Basquiats were on the verge of separation, a further disaster befell Jean-Michel. At the age of seven, whilst playing in the street, he was hit by a car and rushed to hospital where he had his spleen removed. In hospital, Matilde, in an original and inspired gesture, gave Basquiat a copy of *Gray's Anatomy*. He would pore over it and the detailed imagery of the body parts would later be referenced, together with images of cars and ambulances, in much of his work. When Matilde and Gérard separated, Gérard was given custody of the children and moved the family to a comfortable brownstone in Boerum Hill, Brooklyn. Gérard then began dating and would often spend weekends away, with Basquiat having to take charge of his two younger sisters. Basquiat now saw Matilde – who was in and out of psychiatric hospitals – infrequently, usually on a Sunday when she would visit at Boerum Hill, sitting on the outside steps rather than going into the house.

WHAT?
DRAWING OF THE HUMAN BRAIN,
SHOWING MAJOR ARTERIES,
FROM *GRAY'S ANATOMY*.

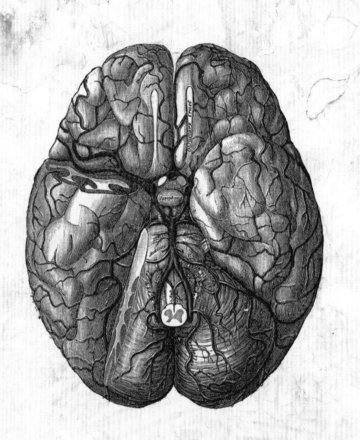

5

ST ANN'S, BROOKLYN HEIGHTS

"Where kids are groomed to be members of the bohemian elite." **Dana Schuster, *Page Six***

Gérard Basquiat wanted the best for his son. In 1971 he put Basquiat in for a scholarship at the chi-chi St Ann's private school in Brooklyn Heights, where Basquiat rubbed shoulders with some of the spoilt children of Wall Street bankers and wealthy Manhattan lawyers. What impact St Ann's had on him is undocumented, but it must have formed a pretty sharp contrast with the public schools that he subsequently attended. What it did give Basquiat was a diverse childhood experience. This wasn't a simple matter of black/ white, but rather an in-built understanding of relative privilege/ hyper privilege, an early education on how to instinctively play the game of ambition and serious success. Basquiat had acquired the idea of 'making it' from a very early age.

WHERE?
SAINT ANN'S SCHOOL,
PIERREPONT STREET,
BROOKLYN HEIGHTS,
NEW YORK CITY.

BASQUIAT'S BROOKLYN

Basquiat's mother, Matilde, the daughter of Puerto Rican parents, grew up in Brooklyn. When she met and married the smart wannabe accountant, Basquiat's father Gérard, they decided to settle in the rather smart Park Slope part of the borough. Difiiculties in their relationship, Matilde's mental illness and their eventual separation meant that the family moved around. For Basquiat, Brooklyn was a place to escape from, to the very happening, but rather dangerous, Manhattan Lower East Side and West Village.

❶ Park Slope
Basquiat birthplace in a comfortable duplex in a handsome brownstone, close to the Park and the Brooklyn Museum.

❷ Flatbush
Basquiat's second home, not as charming as Park Slope, but still a reasonable neighbourhood.

❸ Brooklyn Heights
The smart, upscale end of Brooklyn, with the best views of the Twin Towers the Manhattan skyline. Basquiat attended the private St Ann's School here.

❹ Boerum Hill
Gérard Basquiat bought comfortable, four-storey brownstone here in 1971, where he brought up Basquiat and his two sisters as a single parent. After their return from Puerto Rico, Basquiat went to the school across the street.

Gérard's new found wealth after Basquiat's death in 1988 did not lead to any move to a flashier neighbourhood. He stayed here until he died in 2013.

❺ Bushwick
Matilde Basquiat moved here after the separation, the poorest part of Brooklyn. Visitors described it as the most delapidated house on the street. dolorum dendam re non nus doluptam

❻ Manhattan
Basquiat and his mother Matilde, would make many trips to the Manhattan museums, particularly MoMA and the Met.

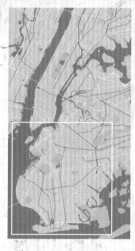

Above: New York City.
Right: Brooklyn (one of the five NYC boroughs) detail.

6

PUERTO RICO

"My mother went crazy as a result of a bad marriage to my father."
Basquiat

The offer of a job at travel publishers Berlitz in Puerto Rico persuaded Gérard Basquiat to move to the Caribbean island when Basquiat was 12. He was already old beyond his years and it was in Puerto Rico that he began experimenting with sex, later suggesting that his first experiences were with men. It must have been strange to be living in his mother's birth place, but with his dad, and to see the contrast between the wealth of Brooklyn Heights and Manhattan and the poverty of much of Puerto Rico. Racism in Puerto Rico was also deeply ingrained in the 1970s, with status being conferred according to the amount of "white blood" in ones makeup, particularly caustic in an environment where most of the population was of mixed ethnicity. This did not politicise Basquiat, but it probably did make him highly conscious, on a personal level, of racial inequality.

WHERE?
BEACH AT SAN JUAN,
PUERTO RICO,
THE CARIBBEAN.

7

WASHINGTON SQUARE PARK

"There was a lot of ugly stuff going on in my family." Basquiat

Basquiat came back from Puerto Rico in a state of rebellion. He attended Edward R. Murrow High School across the road from the Boerum Hill house, but failed every class, including getting the accolade of being the only pupil in his class to fail life drawing. Neighbours noticed a hostile edge to his manner. Then, aged 15, he ran away from home, after Gérard, he claimed, stabbed him "in the ass" when he caught him having sex with his (male) cousin. He shaved his head and went 30 miles outside the City, to Harriman State Park for a few days, and then holed up in a Jewish hippie commune on West 12th Street, before ending up in Washington Square Park, where he spent eight months, "dropping acid." It was a transformative experience. In Washington Square, Basquiat met the graffiti gangs 3YB, SS, The Stone Soul Brothers and MG. They would regularly go and bomb the subway trains. Basquiat didn't join in, but he had hit on a direction for his art. A critical connection was made: here was an aesthetic whose energy he could fashion into something new.

WHO?
BASQUIAT,
WITH MOHICAN HAIRCUT,
C. 1975.

19

8

CITY–AS–SCHOOL

"He told me he had been a [male] prostitute on 42nd Street." Ken Cybulska

Trying to find Baquiat was a nightmare for Gérard. He eventually tracked him down to Washington Square and brought him home. Unbeknownst to Gérard, during his time on the street Basquiat had acquired a serious drug problem: acid, pot and heroin. We don't know whose idea it was, but Basquiat now enrolled at the inspirational City-As-School. It was a perfect fit. The School, run by ex-hippies, was designed for gifted, errant kids. Its central idea was that pupils should go and get steeped in all the energy and culture that New York had to offer. Tokens were provided for access to the major museums. It was here that Basquiat met Al Diaz, a subway train graffiti bomber. They would exchange their tokens for pot and go and hang out in the West Village or Central Park. But they did go to some MoMA classes, and the art teachers, recognising his talent, really encouraged his drawing and writing. But back home relations with his father were deteriorating. Basquiat would usually go and crash with friends: anything to avoid going home.

WHERE?
CITY-AS-SCHOOL,
CLARKSON STREET,
WEST VILLAGE,
MANHATTAN.

9

BIRTH OF SAMO©

"We were smoking some grass one night and I said something about it being the same old shit. SAMO, right?"
Basquiat, interview in *The Village Voice*

The SAMO idea began as a piece for the City–As–School newspaper *Basement Blues Press*. Basquiat and Al Diaz were smoking weed, commenting on how it was the same old shit, and SAMO was shoehorned into the student newspaper issue on alternative religions as a new 'faith'. Basquiat and Diaz developed a logo to go with it and then, rather like Shepard Fairey and OBEY thirty years later, began to bomb the streets with the logo. The SAMO logo was accompanied by a series of statements and by a copyright symbol. They bombed the Brooklyn Bridge, great swathes of Tribeca and SoHo, including the Mary Boone Gallery. The *SoHo News* and *The Village Voice* took notice trying, Banksy-style, to uncover the identity of the perpetrator. Ever the self-publicist, Basquiat sold his story to *The Village Voice* for $100, quickly spent on drugs.

WHERE?
SAMO GRAFFITO,
JONES STREET,
LOWER EAST SIDE,
MANHATTAN.

PERFECT TIMING

Looking back, it all happened so quickly for Basquiat. His timing was impeccable. The Lower East Side, Tribeca and West Village of New York became his stamping ground. Seeing the chi-chi galleries, clubs and designer lofts which characterise these neighbourhoods today, it is hard to imagine the state of near collapse they were in in the late '70s and '80s. Buildings were abandoned, given over to squatters and drug dealers. Crime was rife and the introduction of crack cocaine further exacerbated the cycle of violence and crime. New Yorkers were leaving the city in droves; the Big Apple had become the Rotten Apple. With the City effectively bankrupt, police force budgets were slashed. The subway became an underground hotbed of crime. The annual murder rate reached 2,245. There was no better culture for art to thrive. Artists could live in big spaces without paying rent. Graffiti artists made subway cars their canvases. The downtown punk scene and its successor, new wave, took off in venues like CBGB's. And the clubs were legendary: The Mudd Club, Area – both so much edgier than Studio54. It was a scene, where punk, graffiti, art, jazz, poetry could intermingle and thrive, all laced with coke and heroin. And into this scene stepped Blondie, Bowie, Burroughs, Warhol, Haring, Scharf and, of course Basquiat. Never before, or since, has New York been so dangerous, or so exciting.

BIRD ON MONEY 1981

FISHING 1981

UNTITLED (SKULL) 1981

IRONY OF THE NEGRO
POLICEMAN 1981

ARROZ CON POLLO 1981

CROWNS (PESO NETO) 1981

PER CAPITA 1981

UNTITLED (CAR CRASH) 1981

UNTITLED (BLUE AIRPLANE)
1981

1

SCHOOL OF VISUAL ARTS

"People were more interested in the [graffiti] phenomenon than the art itself."
Keith Haring, *Vogue*

Basquiat didn't bother to finish his senior year at City–As–School. He carried on doing his SAMO tags around lower Manhattan and hanging out around the School of Visual Arts, asking students to sneak him in past the guards with faked teacher notes. It was here that he quickly met Keith Haring and Kenny Scharf and they began hanging out on the streets, Haring doing his hieroglyphics, Scharf his dayglo take on Looney Tune characters and Basquiat SAMO. His timing, fortuitously, was perfect. Critics and journalists had just become fascinated with the explosion in graffiti art, particularly on NYC subway cars; psychologists identified a link between graffiti artists and overbearing fathers; Norman Mailer wrote a book on the movement and then in 1975 the first gallery show was held. Basquiat, to his chagrin, was labelled a 'graffiti artist' along with the rest. He had a different direction in mind.

WHERE?
THE SCHOOL OF VISUAL ARTS,
EAST 23RD STREET,
MANHATTAN.

2

THE MUDD CLUB / GRAY

" A fly-by-night crowd of punks, posers and the ultra hip...flaunt manic chic." **People**

Basquiat had great instinct. Just as he knew the School of Visual Arts was the place to hang during the day, he knew the Mudd Club was the place to be most other times. Opened in a no-go (too dangerous then) part of Tribeca in 1978 by filmmaker Steve Mass, inspired art curator Diego Cortez and punk rock 'It' girl, Anya Phillips, it established itself as the antithesis of glamorous Studio54. Mudd became the destination of choice for the post-CBGB crowd, regulars included Debbie Harry, The Talking Heads, Grace Jones, Mick Jagger, David Bowie, Nico and, occasionally, Andy Warhol. Basquiat's 'bugged-out' robotic dances made an instant impression on the dance floor – "he looked like a Bowery bum and a fashion model at the same time", according to Cortez. Basquiat formed an 'art-noise' band – Gray, after *Gray's Anatomy* – and they regularly performed at the Club. He wrote many song lyrics, the titles of which would later find their way into his paintings. Basquiat was plugged into the coolest crowd in NYC, even if it came at a price: heroin was the Mudd Club's drug of choice, and Basquiat's began experimenting.

WHERE?
BASQUIAT WITH HIS BAND GRAY,
THE MUDD CLUB, 77 WHITE STREET,
TRIBECA,
MANHATTAN.

③

EAST 12TH ST

"The derelict streets of the East Village provided his raw materials."
Alexis Adler

Basquiat, now 18, was living a couch-surfing life, crashing wherever he could, often with girls picked up at the Mudd Club, sometimes with guys. He scrabbled for money and meals. Sometimes he and gay friends would turn tricks around Times Square. He had an affair with Klaus Nomi (who complained that Basquiat had given him gonorrhea four times). Then for six months he dated and stayed with Alexis Adler, who remembers his incredible creative drive. Basquiat couldn't afford canvases, so he acquired anything – old TVs, boxes, crushed briefcases – and fashioned them into art. He would scrawl on the floors and walls of their abandoned apartment, walking around with a small red cassette player playing Bowie's *Heroes* or *Low*. After his Mudd Club sessions, Basquiat would bring Cortez round to look at his scrawls. The uber perceptive Cortez recognised that here was a real talent: "he was a kind of genius, something was going to happen with him."

WHERE?
BASQUIAT AT THE TIME HE LIVED WITH ALEXIS ADLER,
EAST VILLAGE,
MANHATTAN.

(4)

WPA RESTAURANT

"He's too young."
Henry Geldzahler, New York Art Commissioner

The people who knew Basquiat in '78/79 commented on his burning ambition, his sense of destiny, inner spark and intense eyes. He had a conviction that he would be a star and sought to emulate his heroes: Hendrix, Charlie Parker, Billie Holliday, the boxers Sugar Ray Robinson and Joe Louis, and William Burroughs. Basquiat always carried a copy of Burroughs's *Junky* around with him. But his greatest obsession was with Warhol and Basquiat had decided that he would somehow find a way of getting taken up by him. He discovered Warhol liked to lunch at WPA restaurant in SoHo and, with total directness, went up one day whilst Andy was with New York's art commissioner, Henry Geldzahler, and tried to sell one of his postcards. Warhol bought the postcard, but showed no further interest. Geldzahler dismissed Basquiat out of hand. Little did Geldzahler know that in less than two years he would be collecting Basquiat; little did Warhol know that in six years he and Basquiat would be not just collaborating, but working out at the gym together.

WHAT?
SCENE FROM *BASQUIAT* THE MOVIE.
BASQUIAT INTERRUPTING WARHOL'S LUNCH AT
WPA TO SHOW HIM ONE OF HIS POSTCARDS.
GELDZAHLER REJECTS BAQUIAT'S APPROACH.
SOHO, MANHATTAN.

5

THE TIMES SQ SHOW

"The Times Square Show hit like a dose of free-based cocaine." **Peter Frank**

It was in a disused massage parlour in the then porn district of Manhattan that the artists' collective, Colab and Fashion Moda held the ground-breaking Times Square Show. Graffiti as an art movement was born at the show: it was already in the air (*The Village Voice* had just carried a big feature on graffiti), but the mixture of graffiti, feminist artists, punk art, massage parlour dildos and Basquiat, Haring and Scharf proved irresistible to critics. Jeffrey Deitch singled out Basquiat: "he's a knock-out combination of de Kooning and subway spray paint scribbles."

WHERE?
PORN CINEMAS CIRCA 1980,
42 SECOND ST,
TIMES SQUARE,
MANHATTAN.

6

NEW YORK BEAT

"I got into nightclubs before I was even a painter." Basquiat to Anthony Haden-Guest

The downtown music and art scenes were closely, almost incestuously bound together, but it was the new wave music scene that, in 1980, had the greater energy. After the Times Square Show Basquiat was becoming a minor celebrity amongst the Mudd Club crowd but a total unknown elsewhere. But it looked as though this would soon change. Glenn O'Brien, then music columnist on Andy Warhol's *Interview* magazine, was writing about new bands on the scene, and decided to shoot a movie to capture the vibe. He cast Basquiat in the leading role, featuring a homeless artist wandering the streets of Manhattan trying to sell his work and going to see various bands. Debbie Harry played a bag lady, kissed by Basquiat, who turns into a gorgeous princess. Basquiat took up residence in the film's production office, turning it into a temporary studio, and his first canvases were created for the movie. His band Gray also featured. After the shoot, Debbie Harry and Chris Stein bought one of Basquiat's works, for $200. Sadly the production ran out of money and the film wasn't released until 2000, retitled *Downtown 81*.

WHO?
DEBBIE HARRY
AT THE TIME *NEW YORK BEAT* WAS SHOT.

(7)

NEW YORK/NEW WAVE AT P.S.1

"If Cy Twombly and Jean Dubuffet had a baby...it would be Jean-Michel." Art Forum

Diego Cortez (real name Jim Curtis) was the extraordinary impressario of both the Mudd Club and graffiti scenes in NYC, with fingers in so many pies, from music, to indie film, to art. He co-founded Colab and contributed to the Times Square Show. It was at the Mudd Club, on the dance floor, that he met Basquiat, attracted by his blonde mohawk. They became friends and Basquiat began crashing at Cortez's pad on the Lower East Side. Cortez spotted Basquiat's talent and when he decided to curate his PS1 show, Basquiat was one of 119 artists. New York/ New Wave generated huge buzz, with big crowds heading out to Long Island City to see the show which would define a new direction for art. Basquiat's 15 pieces had their own room. All the critics said his was the stand-out work. One piece sold for $2500. NYC Cultural Commissioner Henry Geldzahler now asked to meet Basquiat and bought another piece for $2000. Cortez read the runes: he was already planning to introduce Basquiat to the mega dealer circuit.

WHERE?
THE DISUSED ELEMENTARY SCHOOL WHICH BECAME
THE PS1 CONTEMPORARY ART SPACE,
LONG ISLAND CITY,
QUEENS. NEW YORK.

⑧

MUDD CLUB GALLERY

"Fab 5 Freddy told me everybody's fly."
Blondie 'Rapture'

Fab 5 Freddy was one of the graffiti gang regularly bombing the New York subway. His tag was named after the Lexington Avenue No. 5 train, over which, according to graffiti gang hierarchy, he held certain rights. He had famously created an early link between graffiti and the art world, painting Warholian Campbell's soup cans on a subway train. It was on the fourth floor of the Mudd Club, the art space curated by Keith Haring, that Fab 5 co-curated his Beyond Words show of graffiti-inspired works which included SAMO. The aim of the show was to link the uptown, Bronx rap and graffiti scenes with the downtown SoHo, Tribeca and East Village art and punk/new wave scenes. The show wasn't as big as PS1, but the artworks were being seen by the hippest crowd in the City. Interestingly Basquiat didn't like being labelled a graffiti artist and Diego Cortez commented, on meeting Basquiat (and seeing him dance) at Mudd Club, "he had nothing to do with black culture. He was this Kraftwerkian technocreature, a sort of caricature of the future."

WHO?
FAB 5 FREDDY,
MUDD CLUB,
77 WHITE STREET,
TRIBECA,
MANHATTAN.

RUSH OF SUCCESS

The dealers were already interested in the graffiti movement pouring out of Manhattan downtown. The question was, how to monetize it, how to bring it into the gallery? The smart curation of Cortez and Basquiat's work gave them the answer. After the PS1 show, dealers were all over Basquiat, with Cortez as the conduit: he went straight from scraping a living selling $1 postcards and t-shirts, to making $30,000 a show ($100,000 in today's terms). An Italian dealer gave Basquiat his first show in Modena. In NYC the clever, elegant (and also Italian) Annina Nosei took Basquiat on for her SoHo gallery. Charming but also a very cool operator, she completely understood how Basquiat needed to be treated, giving him a space to work, later paying for his smart loft and showering him with cash. This was a powerful brew for a 21-year old. The cash went straight into drugs, Armani suits, endless limos, and impulsive travel. But Basquiat's work at this time was stunning, still considered by many critics the best of his all too brief career.

BOY AND DOG IN A JOHNNY
JUMP 1982

PROFIT I 1982

CABEZA 1982

SELF-PORTRAIT 1982

OBNOXIOUS LIBERALS 1982

BRETT AS A NEGRO 1982

CASIUS CLAY 1982

ST JOE LOUIS SURROUNDED BY
SNAKES 1982

UNTITLED 1982

SLAVE AUCTION 1982

PORTRAIT OF THE ARTIST AS A
YOUNG DERELICT 1982

UNTITLED 1982

1

MODENA

"You're not going to believe this... I just made $30,000!" Basquiat to Patti Astor

It's hard to imagine a greater contrast between the drug-fuelled, almost abandoned Tribeca and East Village of the 1980s, and the Renaissance elegance of Modena, also home to Ferrari and Lamborghini. The link was the brilliant dealer, Emilio Mazzoli, whose emponymous gallery was behind the Transavantgarde movement. One of his artists, Sandro Chia, put Mazzoli onto Basquiat after the PS1 show. When he was next in Manhattan, Diego Cortez showed him the Basquiat works he had, and he bought $10,000 ($30,000 today) worth on the spot, agreeing to hold Basquiat's first ever solo show at his gallery that May. It was Basquiat's first trip to Europe. Modena freaked him out: pot, LSD and junk food – also hard to find – were the only way he could cope. Mazzoli bought him art supplies, so he could produce more and more work, including big 6-foot canvases. A pattern had been established: dealers inadvertently fuelling Basquiat's drug habit with instant hard cash, which fuelled a fast production of big, brilliant, very tradeable artworks.

WHERE?
PIAZZA GRANDE,
MODENA,
ITALY.

2

ANNINA NOSEI

"It was the first time I had a place to work."
Basquiat

Whilst Basquiat was in Modena, dealers in New York were already circling, waiting to pick up Basquiat on his return. Diego Cortez was making those connections happen. In June 1981 Annina Nosei, an Italian dealer who had opened her gallery in SoHo in 1979, and whose artists included Sandro Chia and Francesco Clemente, ran into Cortez in Berlin and they discussed Basquiat. By September she had recruited him to her stable, offering him wads of cash for art supplies and, inevitably, drugs. She paid for his hotel rooms at the Martha Washington Hotel on West 23rd St. She suggested he come and work in her basement. Basquiat, in short, was given total security. Dropping the SAMO© tag, Annina offered works by her new star, 'Basquiat', to existing influential collectors. Basquiat was now hanging next to uber established names: Rauschenberg, La Salle, Kruger. It was, in an echo of Wall Street bond traders in the early '80s, an instant rush to making it. Everyone now wanted a piece of Basquiat and Basquiat, now with the new high of success to keep chasing, was happy to provide.

WHERE?
SCENE FROM THE MOVIE BASQUIAT.
THE ARTIST, *BASQUIAT*, PORTRAYED CREATING IN
THE NOSEI GALLERY'S BASEMENT,
100 PRINCE STREET, SOHO.

③

WEST 23RD STREET

"Whenever I got a new shipment of coke I would invite [Basquiat] to come over and taste test it." **Jeffrey Bretschneider**

Jeffrey Bretschneider ran a kind of salon from his apartment on 23rd Street, next to the Chelsea Hotel. It was here that Basquiat acquired most of his coke and where, after the Mudd Club or Club 57, he would come and hang out with the regulars: Debbie Harry, Chris Stein, Billy Idol, Fab 5 Freddy. Basquiat's first show at Annina Nosei's – The Public Address Show, also with Keith Haring, Barbara Kruger and Jenny Holzer – was a big success. Annina Nosei now upped the ante. Even though Basquiat would only show up to 'the dungeon' in the afternoon, he would then work at speed, piles of coke spilling everywhere. Annina started selling works even before they were finished. Diego Cortez wasn't impressed: having a black artist producing work in a basement and bringing 'suburban white folk' down to observe 'the freak circus person' had bad overtones. Basquiat was hyper, but he knew what he was doing. "He was having a good time", according to Glenn O'Brien.

WHERE?
WEST 23RD STREET,
CHELSEA,
MANHATTAN,
NYC.

④

CULEBRA

"I'm going to make you the most famous painter in America." Rene Ricard, art critic

The arrangement with Nosei got Basquiat working at a rate of knots, including creating one of his breakthrough works, *Arroz con Pollo*. Close to burn out he asked for some time off. In almost parental fashion, Annina gave Basquiat some holiday funds. Basquiat took off to Puerto Rico, with a new Mudd Club girlfriend, Valda Grinfelds, to stay with Leisa Stroud. Rene Ricard, the art critic who had discovered Basquiat by chance after seeing one of his paintings in Maripol's, the Fiorucci art director's loft, turned up also. But Basquiat didn't come to chillout. He brought several rolled up canvases with him, including *Arroz con Pollo*, which he reworked a number of times. It's a work that evokes Picasso in its rawness; a depiction of a chicken dinner Leisa, Basquiat, Valda and Rene had on Culebra, featuring a black figure looking away, serving a charred chicken to a white figure presenting her breast and vulva in exchange. One can see why the dealers and critics went crazy: Basquiat was producing works of total sophistication, at the age of just 21.

WHERE?
BEACH AT CULEBRA,
PUERTO RICO.

5

101 CROSBY STREET

"He would buy all these Armani and Versace suits, paint in them and then throw them away." **Suzanne Mallouk**

After the success of the Public Address Show, Annina Nosei further protected her investment by installing Basquiat in his own loft around the corner from the gallery. Here he had enough room to paint in his own place, free-basing cocaine. Suzanne Mallouk, an ex, reappeared and moved in, but Basquiat's escalating coke habit was making him paranoid, unpredictable and occasionally violent. Basquiat now hired an assistant/ bouncer, Stephen Torton, who also began building stretchers for his canvases from found materials – a Basquiat innovation. The work rate was prodigious – "five paintings for five days, then he'd sleep for a week" according to Mallouk. He would spend the big chunks of cash from Nosei immediately, compulsively, on the suits, the limos, the travel. He took off for Paris with a stunning model for Valentino, returning two weeks later, with a new habit: snorting heroin. It was convenient that Torton also dealt in the stuff. Mallouk decided to move out.

WHERE?
CROSBY STREET,
SOHO,
MANHATTAN.

6

CHARLIE 'BIRD' PARKER

"Bird was the first jazz musician who carried the battle to the enemy." **Ross Russell**

Basquiat was obsessed with music and amassed a collection of over 3000 albums; music was always blasting out when he worked. Favourites included Curtis Mayfield, Bach, David Byrne, Beethoven, Bowie (specifically *Low*), Miles Davis, Donna Summer and Public Image but, most of all, Charlie Parker. Whilst growing up, and later in the downtown arts scene, Basquiat had few black friends. He was the perennial outsider. It was Gérard who introduced him to jazz, but Basquiat made Parker – "the first angry black man in music" – his own personal idol, probably the artist he most identified with. The '©' symbol attached to Basquiat's SAMO© tags may have been inspired by the way Parker was ripped off by white record companies for not properly copyrighting his work. References to Parker appear frequently in his paintings, notably in *Charles the First* and *Bird on Money*. The similarities between Basquiat and Parker are striking: both innovative geniuses in their genres; both black, in businesses where the whites held all the cards; both self-destructive heroin addicts, also seeking escape in sex; and both died young in New York: Basquiat at 27, Parker at 34.

WHO?
CHARLIE 'BIRD' PARKER,
PLAYING AT THE THREE DEUCES AGED 27,
WEST 52ND STREET, NEW YORK, IN 1947.

BASQUIAT'S MANHATTAN

When Basquiat ran away from home aged 15, he ended up in Washington Square Park. He then attended City-As-School, and began to frequent clubs and scenes in then delapidated SoHo and Tribeca. He never wandered far from this stamping ground. His main gallerists – Annina Nosei and, later, Mary Boone – were here and he lived close by, first at a loft in Crosby Street paid for by Nosei, and later in a building owned by Andy Warhol. The East Village was also where he would go an score his drugs, although later the dealers came to him. Basquiat died from an overdose in 1988, in the Great Jones Street loft.

1 **Washington Sq Park** Basquiat lived rough here in 1975.

2 **City-as-School, 16 Clarkson St.** Basquiat attended in 1976.

3 **The Mudd Club, 77 White St.** Basquiat, a regular, whose band Gray played here, first also met Diego Cortez here in 1978.

4 **East 12th St.** Basquiat lived here with Alexis Adler in 1978.

5 **Annina Nosei, 100 Prince St.** Basquiat's first gallery. He worked in the basement in 1981.

6 **151 Crosby St.** Basquiat lived here in 1982-83.

7 **Fun Gallery, 254 E10th St.** Basquiat exhibited here in 1982.

8 **Mary Boone Gallery, 417 West Broadway** Boone became Basquiat's main US dealer in 1984.

9 **Area Club, 157 Hudson St.** Basquiat met Jennifer Goode here in 1984.

10 **Shafrazi Gallery, 163 Mercer St.** Site of the ill-fated Basquiat–Warhol collaborations show in 1985.

11 **222 Bowery** Basquiat meets Burroughs here in 1986.

12 **Cable Building, 611 Broadway** Basquiat has his last show here in 1988.

13 **Great Jones St.** Basquiat lived here from 1984 until his death in 1988.

⑦

GAGOSIAN

"[Gagosian] ...a symbol of the bullish 1980s, when artworks were traded like Wall Street commodities." **The New York Times**

Larry Gagosian had never heard of Basquiat when he showed up at Annina Nosei's Public Address Show. A shiver, he later said, went down his spine when he saw the Basquiats: he bought several on the spot. He then started buying directly from Basquiat in Crosby Street, to Nosei's chagrin, but they remained on good enough terms that they organised Basquiat's first L.A. show together, in April 1982. Basquiat flew out, with his old graffiti gang: Rammellzee, Toxic, A-1 and the ubiquitous Fab 5 Freddy, all paid for by Gagosian. On the flight, Basquiat produced a big bag of coke, which they proceeded to snort. When the stewardess remonstrated that this was illegal, Basquiat rejoindered: "but I thought this was First Class?" Basquiat was late for the opening, headed to the back room to smoke pot, and refused to remove his headphones to talk to the assembled L.A. art world aristocracy. They of course loved the bad-boy behaviour: the show was a sell-out.

WHO?
LARRY GAGOSIAN, THE PROTOTYPICAL
1980S DEALER. HE HAD GALLERIES IN
NEW YORK AND L.A.

8

CHATEAU MARMONT

"He never went to the beach, he would just go to nightclubs and then sleep."
Stephen Torton

After the success of the show, Basquiat decided to stay in California, holing up in Bungalow 3 at the legendary Chateau Marmont hotel, where John Belushi had died after speedballing. A sense of irony was not lost on Basquiat; at the time it seemed funny. Gagosian arranged for a limo to be available for Basquiat and the many friends he chose to fly out. They would cruise around L.A., going from club to club. Many times they were stopped by the LAPD, who refused to believe they weren't drug dealers, but somehow they never got busted. There was little evidence of work whilst Basquiat was in California. When he went back to New York in August 1982, it was to sever ties with Nosei. She was in Europe, so Basquiat and Torton went into the basement of the gallery, identified which canvases were still his, and, high on dope, proceeded to slash them with knives, leaving them in a pile on the floor and throwing a bucket of paint over them. It was a necessary, if childish, rebellion against the dealer system and its controlling nature.

WHERE?
CHATEAU MARMONT HOTEL,
SUNSET BOULEVARD,
WEST HOLLYWOOD.

BOOM BOOM BOOM

As the 1980s art market gathered pace, so did Basquiat's success. Newly minted Wall Street millionaires, slavishly obeying Gordon Gekko's 'Greed is Good' mantra, wanted to invest in 'shock of the new' art. These new Masters of the Universe were hungry for stuff to hang in their cool, interior-designed lofts: to display having made it, "even the rawest junk bond trillionaire knows that art is the best way", Robert Hughes observed. The prospect of being immortalised by gifting to the major museums played their part. Collectors were becoming addicts for art, and the dealers who supplied their next fix held the power. For Basquiat this meant more money and a new international mega dealer, the unlikely figure of Bruno Bischofberger. Basquiat now also had a stable of hyper-wealthy collectors. More money, more girlfriends (including Madonna), more limos, more drugs. The work – still brilliant (*Florence*, of 1983, perhaps a high point) – kept pouring out. But Basquiat's habit was starting to get out of control. Yet, in the midst of this whirlwind, Basquiat achieved a long-held ambition by properly meeting Warhol.

DOS CABEZAS 1982

OFFENSIVE ORANGE 1982

BAPTISMAL 1982

HORN PLAYERS 1983

NAPOLEONIC STEREOTYPE 1983

HISTORY OF THE BLACK PEOPLE
1983

FLORENCE 1983

IN ITALIAN 1983

DISCOGRAPHY (ONE) 1983

BROTHER'S SAUSAGE 1983

RED SAVOY 1983

BRUNO BISCHOFBERGER

"[Basquiat] was just one of those kids who drove me crazy....Bruno discovered him and now he's on Easy Street." Andy Warhol

Bruno Bischofberger, the Swiss mega art dealer (and one of a handful of people to have won a dozen races on the Cresta Run) had been circling Basquiat after seeing his work at New York/ New Wave. He was responsible (aged 24) for bringing Pop Art – Warhol, Lichtenstein, Johns, Oldenburg – to Europe. Twice a month he would fly Concorde to NYC to buy artists' work to ship to Europe. Now, with Annina out of the picture, he persuaded Basquiat to make him his international dealer. He gave Basquiat a one man show at his gallery in Zürich in September '82 but, more importantly, he catalysed a lunch meeting with Warhol at The Factory in New York that October. Following the lunch, Basquiat rushed off and produced a dual portrait of him and Warhol – *Dos Cabezas* – delivered two hours later. Basquiat's admiration was a given, but now that his pictures were selling in Zürich and Düsseldorf for $20,000+, Warhol too was suddenly rather interested in this rising star.

WHERE?
BRUNO IN HIS APPENZELL OUTFIT
IN HIS GALLERY IN ZÜRICH.

2

GIRLFRIENDS

"He had the presence of a movie star and I was crazy about him."
Madonna on Basquiat in *The Guardian*

Basquiat, not hugely tall at 5ft 10", but athletic, graceful and with a touch of little boy charm, knew how attractive he was. He was always surrounded by potential lovers, men and women. There were a few early relationships before Paige Powell and Jennifer Goode. Eszter Balint was a young actress, a regular at the Mudd Club, whom he dated in 1980. He moved on from her to Suzanne Mallouk, tall, half-Palestinian, who he met in Night Birds bar and whose Crosby Street loft he moved into. She got fed up with his 'childlike, bum' ways and moved out. In 1981 he had an intense, brief affair with a fellow artist Patti Anne Blau, then Mallouk came back on the scene. In 1982 he met Madonna at Bowlmor bowling alley. They seemed similar, both hyper-driven. She moved in and out of Crosby Street and they went to L.A. together for eight weeks. But deep down they were very different: Madonna was ultra-organised, into health and fitness, and she didn't do drugs. She decamped to New York, back to Jellybean Benitez. Basquiat was temporarily distraught.

WHO?
MADONNA, CIRCA 1982.

FUN GALLERY

"I'm not doing this East Village shit! I'm outta here. I'm at the Whitney."
Basquiat to Patti Astor

The first gallery in the East Village, devoted to graffiti artists, was founded by Patti Astor and Bill Stelling. Bischofberger was against Basquiat showing there – his stock was now riding too high – but somehow he was persuaded. His prices were much reduced: $6000 to $10,000. The opening was a huge success, with all of New York's top collectors mixing it with graffiti street kids who a few hours earlier might have been bombing subway cars. Basquiat was in Armani, chaperoned by Madonna. Celebrities turned up – Paul Simon tried to buy a picture but was outbid. Bischofberger grandly appeared in his big Merc and, to his surprise, loved it: "I think it was the greatest show of his life...I went about 12 times...the opening was great too, a mixture of street kids and elegant people." Even Annina Nosei appeared: she bought a work for $7500 and sold it a few days later for $15,000. Many thought that Basquiat had reclaimed his credibility, but he was bitter, claiming: "I never got paid...it was so unprofessional it was sickening."

WHAT?
A GRAFFITI-BOMBED NYC SUBWAY CAR,
C. 1982.

④

ST MORITZ

"I have to go to St Moritz to see my dealer, he's kind of a shark but he's a good shark."
Basquiat to Brook Bartlett

It was somewhat incongruous that of all his dealers, Basquiat stayed longest with Bruno Bischofberger. The son of the Zürich doctor, who found it amusing to wear Appenzell peasant garb, whose first love was collecting Swiss folk art and who counted the Agnellis, Stavros Niarchos and Gunter Sachs as friends, he managed to hold onto Basquiat from 1982-1987. With great prescience, Bischofberger had built a chalet on his property in St Moritz to serve as an artist's studio, to prompt visiting artists to knock out new work. Basquiat was flown over and made use of it on several occasions, but also began treating the Bischofbergers as a surrogate family, hanging out with their three children, and inviting himself over for Christmas. Yet there was no let up in the drug use. Even with the family, Basquiat would regularly be conked out, one Christmas even refusing to come out of his room and then, when reprimanded, escaping in a sulk by cab to Zürich. Cool as ever, Bischofberger wasn't fazed, as long as Basquiat kept the paintings coming.

WHERE?
BASQUIAT AT WORK IN ST MORITZ,
ENGADIN VALLEY.

5

THE WHITNEY

"The show is just like the Sixties...these kids are selling everything." Andy Warhol

Basquiat had started 1983, literally and metaphorically, on a high. His solo show of 25 paintings at Gagosian in March was a triumph of celebrity and critical reaction; according to Jeff Bretschneider "it was not about what work was on the walls, but which people were in the room." That same month the Whitney included two Basquiats – *Dutch Settlers* and *Untitled (Skull)* – in their Biennial. Just as he had predicted, Basquiat had made it into a major American museum. He was just 22. In 1983 Wall Street was on a roll and the art market also on a high. After an ecclectic period, there was a sense that a major new art movement – Neo-Expressionism – was in full flow, with Basquiat as one of its leading exponents. Auction prices started escalating and collectors were spending again. The term 'art-lust' was coined to describe the mood and Basquiat's timing couldn't have been better. As if to cement the year, at the Whitney Basquiat was to meet his next New York dealer, the uber cool and knowing Mary Boone.

WHERE?
THE WHITNEY MUSEUM OF AMERICAN ART,
MADISON AVENUE AND 75TH STREET,
UPPER EAST SIDE,
MANHATTAN.

TRAVELS AND SHOWS 1981–1983

Basquiat's very first solo show was in Modena, Italy, at the Mazzoli Gallery. This was followed by hugely succesful shows at the Annina Nosei Gallery in New York. The Los Angeles shows – which were all sold out – were at the Larry Gagosian Gallery. When Bruno Bischofberger became Basquiat's interntional dealer, he would travel frequently to Zurich. Basquiat tended to also make impulsive trips abroad – in this period to Jamaica with friends and to Madrid and Milan with Warhol. The trip to Tokyo was his first to Japan.

KEY

- ● Travel and Show attended by artist
- ● Show not attended by artist
- ● Travel only

NEW YORK

❷ LOS ANGELES
April 1982
Basquiat's solo show at the Gagosian Gallery.

❻ LOS ANGELES
December 1982–March 1983.
Basquiat in L.A.. Stays at L'Ermitage. Befriends Michael and Tina Chow. Second show at Gagosian.

⑪ LOS ANGELES
Deccmber.
Basquiat and Madonna stay at L'Ermitage. Basquiat rents studio in Venice.

❼ JAMAICA
May 1983
Basquiat travels with Toxic and Nick Taylor.

❺ ROTTERDAM
December 1982
Solo show at Galerie Delta.

❸ KASSEL, GERMANY
June 1982
Documenta 7 show featuring Basquiat works alongside Beuys, Kiefer, Richter, Twombly and Warhol.

NEW YORK SHOWS
1. New York/ New Wave at PS1, organised by Diego Cortez. Feb., 1981.
2. Beyond Words at the Mudd Club. May 1981.
3. Public Address Show at Annina Nosei. Sept., 1981.
4. Solo show at Annina Nosei. March 1982.
5. Fun Gallery solo show. Nov., 1982.
6. Annina Nosei show. March, 1983.
7. Basquiat shown at Whitney. March, 1983.
8. Private show at Paige Powell's apartment. Apr., 1983.

❹ ZURICH
September 1982
Solo show at Bruno Bischofberger.

❾ ZURICH
October 1983
Basquiat stays with Bischofberger.

❶ MODENA
May 1981

Basquiat's first solo show.

❿ TOKYO
October 1983
Basquiat travels with Bischofberger, Show at the Akira Ikeda Gallery.

❽ MILAN AND MADRID
October 1983

Basquiat travels with Warhol.

WARHOL AT LAST

If it was Bruno Bischofberger who effected the Basquiat-Warhol connection, it was Basquiat's girlfriend Paige Powell who proved the catalyst that cemented their friendship. Warhol now developed a personal, prurient interest in Basquiat, as one more character he could gossip about on the phone to his assistant, Pat Hackett, for her to transcribe for his *Diaries*. Bischofberger came up with the idea of collaborative paintings, initially involving Francesco Clemente but later just Warhol and Basquiat. Basquiat, in thrall to Warhol, and seeking his validation, began to think of the master as a father figure. Warhol took the risk of injecting some young serum into his work. The relationship was between a bromance and something quasi-sexual, certainly not consummated. Having separated from the Annina Nosei gallery, Basquiat was now taken up, not without trepidation, by Mary Boone for her SoHo gallery – perhaps the hippest in town. Then, in 1984, Basquiat met Jennifer Goode, and began the most significant emotional relationship of his life.

TOUSSAINT L'OUVERTURE VERSUS
SAVONAROLA 1983

LYE 1983

GRILLO 1984

FLEXIBLE 1984

AUTOPORTRAIT 1984

GOLD GRIOT 1984

PEZ DISPENSER 1984

ZYDECO 1984

OP-OP (WITH WARHOL) 1984

EIFFEL TOWER (WITH WARHOL)
1985

ARM AND HAMMER II (WITH
WARHOL) 1984

PETER AND THE WOLF 1985

ANTHONY CLARKE 1985

①

WEST 81ST ST

"Jean-Michel is really on heroin... he got a hole in his nose and couldn't do coke any more." Andy Warhol

Paige Powell, from a moneyed family and with a cool flat on the Upper West Side, was the advertising director of *Interview* magazine. More importantly, she was close to Warhol. She became Basquiat's lover, quasi manager and also held a show for him in her apartment. It was a smart affair, attended by Schnabel, Clemente and mega collectors like Morton Neumann. Powell became the catalyst of Warhol and Basquiat's connection; it became a ménage-à-trois friendship, with Basquiat moving in with Powell, but spending a lot of time with Andy and his uber celebrity friends. She was in love, but finding it impossible to deal with Basquiat's now serious heroin use. Powell even went on holiday together with Basquiat and his dad, when she decided to tell Gérard that his son was a heroin addict. Basquiat was furious, but they continued to see each other for the next two years, hard not to, given how close Basquiat was now getting to Warhol.

WHO?
PAIGE POWELL,
PICTURED WITH ICE T.

②

GREAT JONES STREET

"I got scared...he's rented our building... what if he's a flash in the pan, and doesn't... pay his rent?" **Andy Warhol**

As Basquiat discovered, it could take a while to pique Andy Warhol's interest. But once done, he could quickly develop a fascination. As Bob Colacello put it "part of Andy saw you as another item in his diary, another tape." As ever, Basquiat's timing was perfect. Warhol and his lover Jon Gould were cooling, and Basquiat filled the gap. The relationship was not consummated, but Warhol did develop a voyeuristic interest in Basquiat's 'big schlong' and would ask Basquiat at dinners "how many times did you come last night?" He also liked Basquiat's style: self-possessed, black, drug addict and successful. For Warhol this was cool, and great diary material. In August he suggested to Basquiat that he move into one of Warhol's properties, a spacious duplex loft on Great Jones Street. He didn't stint on the rent: a punchy $4000 a month. But for Basquiat this would mean he could cement his closeness to Warhol, and in any case Bischofberger offered to cover the cost. All Basquiat had to do was produce regular work, fast.

WHERE?
BASQUIAT, WARHOL AND TINA CHOW, AT HER'S AND
MICHAEL'S EPONYMOUS RESTAURANT,
C. 1983.

③

MICHAEL STEWART

"It was like it could have been him.
It showed him how vulnerable he was."
Keith Haring

Michael Stewart was an aspiring artist, two years older than Basquiat, also from Brooklyn and the boyfriend of his ex, Suzanne Mallouk. On September 15th, 1983, he was picked up by the NYPD for spraying graffiti on a subway wall. After being bludgeoned and left in a coma, he was taken to Bellevue Hospital where he later died. Basquiat was totally traumatised by the news. The reality of what it meant to be a young black man in NYC could not have been more starkly exposed. That night he painted red and black skulls and later illustrated the scene in his work *Untitled (Defacement)*. The work spoke eloquently about the horror he felt, but strangely, when Suzanne Mallouk tried to raise funds to bring the NYPD officers to trial, Basquiat, unlike Haring, contributed nothing. His criticism of racism in the NYPD in his images couldn't have been clearer, yet, when it came to practical action, he was strangely withdrawn. Instead of helping out, Basquiat ran away to Milan with Warhol. In 1985 the NYPD officers concerned were acquitted – surprise, surprise – by an all-white jury.

WHO?
MICHAEL STEWART
SHORTLY BEFORE HIS DEATH IN 1983.

4

COLLABORATIONS

"Jean-Michel came over to the office to paint but he fell asleep on the floor. He looked like a bum...I woke him...he did two masterpieces that were great." Warhol

Bruno Bischofberger was always thinking of the next angle. Basquiat and Warhol – both his artists – were getting close (to the point that they would go and work out together in the gym and then go and get their nails done); what if Basquiat collaborated with Warhol and maybe Clemente too? The three artists created 15 works, first shown at Bruno's Zürich gallery in September. But Warhol and Basquiat had also started collaborating *à deux* in secret at The Factory. The paintings were a somewhat facile mixture of Warhol's logos and Basquiat's word play. Warhol was finding collaborating with Basquiat difficult: whilst he had a rigid 'go to work' ethic, Basquiat would roll up late in the afternoon, totally out of it on heroin – he had a 'non routine'. Dangerously for Basquiat, he was starting to think of Warhol as a father figure, the person he went to for affirmation. Warhol was OK to play along for a while. But emotionally it was Basquiat who was vulnerable.

WHERE?
WARHOL AND BASQUIAT POSING IN FRONT OF
TWO OF THEIR COLLABORATIONS,
SOHO, MANHATTAN.

⑤

MARY BOONE

"I had reservations about making art a business...but I got over it."
Mary Boone to *Life* magazine

Very much the 'It' girl of the '80s art scene, Mary Boone was the incredibly driven gallerist for Julian Schnabel, but also a party girl whose social exploits were brilliant press fodder. Like Basquiat her timing was perfect – she opened her first gallery just as the '80s art and financial boom were about to happen. She agreed to take Basquiat on somewhat reluctantly (she was perceptive about, and cautious of, his chaotic life and drug use) at Bischofberger's suggestion. Basquiat had his first show with her in May 1984, and it was a triumph. Everyone was there for the opening. The fact that Warhol stood very visibly by the entrance for the length of the show, was a sign of how Basquiat was now in blue-chip territory. Boone then managed to secure a cover story for Basquiat in *New York Times Magazine*. If one were to identify a peak in Basquiat's career, this was probably it. But insiders, including Boone, were conscious that artistically he was on the slide. A second show in 1985 was less critically successful and prices were going soft too.

WHERE?
MARY BOONE C. 1984.
HER GALLERY WAS THEN AT 417 WEST BROADWAY,
SOHO, MANHATTAN.

6

AREA

"The whole point of Area was its impermanence."
Eric Goode, *New York Magazine*

In 1984, Area was the happening club in NYC. Basquiat of course was there; Francesco Clemente, Andy Warhol, Keith Haring, Bianca Jagger, Grace Jones and Sting were regulars. The club was renowned for its mad themes, occupying glass cases along its 100-foot entrance, and in charge of the themes was Jennifer Goode, the sister of the two founders. Basquiat met her on the door one evening, started showering her with gifts and she soon started spending time at the Great Jones Street loft. Goode was to become his most important relationship. She did not resist his heroin use, but joined him on the journey. She was deeply in love, but realised after a couple of years that she had to get off the drug. She became pregnant, but the drugs also informed her decision to have an abortion. Goode persuaded Basquiat to join her on a methadone programme, but he quit after a few days. She stuck with it, but eventually ended the relationship in 1987.

WHERE?
BASQUIAT DJ-ING AT AREA,
157 HUDSON STREET,
TRIBECA,
MANHATTAN.

BOOM TO BUST

The fall was very swift. Basquiat was still hugely fêted, but insiders realised that the quality of his work just wasn't as raw or as good. He still scored high on the cool meter: Steve Rubell and Ian Schrager of Studio 54 fame picked Basquiat to paint two murals for the VIP Michael Todd Room at Palladium, their new club, where art was a critical part of the experience. Then in 1985 the Warhol-Basquiat collaborations were exhibited at the Tony Shafrazi Gallery, to general derision from the press. Basquiat's fragile ego couldn't cope. Ever since his SAMO© days his rise had been stratospheric, success piled on success. In his somewhat paranoid state, everything now seemed to be falling apart. It would all end tragically.

ABORIGINAL 1984

FLEXIBLE 1984

RIDDLE ME THIS, BATMAN 1987

VICTOR 1987

TO BE TITLED 1987

UNTITLED 1987

UNBREAKABLE 1987

THE DINGOES THAT PARK THEIR
BRAINS WITH THEIR GUM 1988

EROICA I 1988
EROICA II 1988

EXU 1988

RIDING WITH DEATH 1988

①

PALLADIUM

"Palladium is uptown meets downtown. The artists are the rock stars of the '80s."
Steve Rubell

Ian Schrager and Steve Rubell were the naughty-boy founders of Studio 54. In 1980 they were done for tax evasion and spent 14 months inside, before returning to Manhattan in triumph to open their new club, Palladium. Given the pumping mid-80s mood, they decided that it wasn't enough to have a space designed by Arata Isozaki, they also needed big art. Schnabel, Clemente, Haring and Scharf were all commissioned, but it was Basquiat who was asked to paint the iconic mural behind the Michael Todd Room bar. It got rave reviews, with the *New Yorker* calling Basquiat "the Wunderkind of Neo-expressionism." But Basquiat was now in a bad place. Despite earning a reputed $1 million per year from Boone (rising one time to $4 million), with a suite at the Ritz-Carlton paid for by the gallery, he was falling out with her and the controlling demands of the gallery system. His heroin use was intensifying, and his paranoia also. He also wasn't looking great: dark spots started appearing on his face, most probably caused by toxins from his drug abuse.

WHERE?
BASQUIAT AT PALLADIUM,
14TH STREET,
MANHATTAN.

2

LES BAINS DOUCHES

"He was drawing the whole way...he could throw up something in 10 minutes...like a masterpiece." **Leonard de Knegt**

The relationship with Boone may have been splintering, but the pace for Basquiat didn't let up. His ability to act on impulse was undiminished. On meeting photographer Michael Halsband at a dinner, Basquiat suggested he do a joint Basquiat-Warhol photo, then invited him to Europe, paying for everything. In Paris they went to parties, where everyone was shooting heroin, and then to nightclubs, mostly Les Bains Douches. At a party at George Condo's apartment, the m.o. was snorting coke off the glass of some Picasso framed drawings whilst listening to Hendrix and Miles Davis. They hired a limo and drove to Lisbon. Halsband found the pace, the drugs too much, and headed home, but then returned for another road trip: Lisbon, Paris, Rome, Florence. Basquiat then headed to St Moritz, before being joined by Leonard de Knegt for another limo trip: Portofino, Carrara, Florence, then train to Amsterdam. With no warning Basquiat then disappeared, back to New York.

WHERE?
THE HAPPENING LES BAINS DOUCHES
NIGHTCLUB – 'THE STUDIO 54 OF PARIS',
3RD ARRONDISSEMENT,
PARIS.

②

SHAFRAZI GALLERY

"The collaboration looks like one of Warhol's manipulations...Basquiat comes across as the...accessory." **The NY Times**

Halsband's photo of Warhol and Basquiat in Everlast boxing gear was a classic, showing Warhol in pugilistic and Basquiat in defensive mode, and would be used for the poster of their joint show at Tony Shafrazi's Gallery in September 1985. Warhol, perceptive as ever, had premonitions about the show. He was right to: it was almost universally panned; only one picture sold. The *New York Times* dismissed Basquiat as Warhol's 'mascot'. Basquiat was devastated and turned on Andy. He couldn't bear criticism and, with displaced logic, held his father figure responsible. He dropped Warhol and stopped returning his calls. Bischofberger got caught in the crossfire – Basquiat began complaining about their financial arrangement. His relationship with Paige Powell also collapsed. She had decided to get treatment for her addictions and, according to Warhol, was also dismissive about Basquiat modelling for a Comme des Garçons show. She was over him. Basquiat was losing his grip; his sense of cool was no longer bullet-proof.

WHERE?
TONY SHAFRAZI GALLERY,
163 MERCER STREET,
SOHO, MANHATTAN.

TONY SHAFRAZI ★ BRUNO BISCHOFBERGER

★ PRESENT ★

WARHOL ★ BASQUIAT

PAINTINGS

SEPTEMBER 14 THROUGH OCTOBER 19, 1985

163 MERCER STREET NEW YORK 212 925-8732

③

ABIDJAN

"It was not the man in the street who got to see Jean-Michel's work."
Bruno Bischofberger

The press dropped Basquiat like old news. Having been all over the gossip columns, he was now invisible. Basquiat became more and more withdrawn, staying in with Jennifer Goode in the Great Jones Street Loft, shooting speedballs. Even his dealers thought he looked shocking – he had gum disease, he had lost a front tooth and the blotches on his face were getting worse, some turning to sores. Rumours began to circulate that he had AIDS. Was Basquiat's idea to travel to Africa and have a show an attempt to experience a reality as divorced from celebrity Manhattan as possible? Or – he had at times ascribed the reception of his Shafrazi show as racist at core – was he trying to find some connection with his distant roots? When he arrived in Abidjan, with Jennifer Goode, he was disappointed – he had wanted ordinary Africans to see his work, but it was mostly government flunkies. He returned to New York, to a final break with Mary Boone.

WHERE?
CLOTHES WASHING IN A RIVER OUTSIDE ABIDJAN,
CÔTE D'IVOIRE,
WEST AFRICA.

TRAVELS AND SHOWS 1984–1987

In retrospect, Basquiat had probably reached a peak in 1983. There were more successful shows in Europe and Japan, but in New York the shows with his new dealer, Mary Boone, received less ecstatic reviews. The Shafrazi show received poor reviews. Basquiat made two significant trips, to Hawaii with his father and Jennifer Goode, and then to Abidjan. Both were associated with an attempt to detox and, in the case of Abidjan, a search for his deeper roots in Africa, investigating a possible new direction for his art and life.

KEY
- Travel and Show attended by artist
- Show not attended by artist
- Travel only

① MAUI, HAWAII
January 1984
Basquiat rents a ranch in Hana Joined by Jennifer Goode and his father, amongst others.

⑥ LOS ANGELES
January 1986
Basquiat last show at Gagosian Gallery.

⑦ ABIDJAN, COTE D'IVOIRE.
August 1986
Basquiat, Jennifer Goode and her brother Eric travel to show organised by Bischofberger.

❷ EDINBURGH
August 1984
Basquiat show at
fruitmarket Gallery.

❾ HAMBURG
November 1986
Basquiat contributes to
Luna Luna amusement
park. Other artists include
Dali, Haring, Hockney and
Lichenstein.

❽ HANNOVER
November 1986
Solo show of 60 works at
Kestner–Gesellschaft.

❸ ZURICH 1
September 1984
Basquiat collaborative
paintings, with Warhol
and Clemente, show at
Bischofberger.

❹ ZURICH 2
January 1985
Basquiat one man show
at Bischofberger.

❿ PARIS
January 1987
Basquiat solo show at
Galerie Daniel Templon.

❺ TOKYO
December 1985
Basquiat solo show at
Akira Ikeda Gallery.

④

222 BOWERY

"For Jean-Michel meeting Burroughs was like Andy meeting Muhammad Ali."
Victor Bockris

From his days at City-As-School, Basquiat had carried a copy of William Burroughs's *Junky*, a sort of personal bible and talisman. The prospect of meeting the man himself – Basquiat idolised him still – was hugely exciting. The meeting was arranged by Victor Bockris, Factory regular and contributor to *Interview*. Burroughs was staying at 222 Bowery and met Basquiat together with Keith Haring and John Giorno. According to Bockris, Basquiat was like a child with delight. Burroughs, Giorno and Basquiat then headed back to Basquiat's loft, to speedballs. Giorno was amazed at the amount of heroin lying around, little bags piled into a small mountain. But the meeting produced nothing. Basquiat's work was now obviously suffering – he was producing much less and of inferior quality. Goode, realising that she could change nothing, and constantly terrified that she would come home to find Basquiat dead from an overdose, decided to leave the relationship, but to remain a friend. Basquiat was both devastated and in denial.

WHO?
WILLIAM BURROUGHS, C. 1982.

⑤

WARHOL R.I.P.

"The death of Warhol made the death of Basquiat inevitable, somehow..."
Donald Rubell

If Jennifer Goode leaving was a terrible blow for Basquiat, Warhol's unexpected death on the 22nd February 1987, following a routine gall bladder operation, was completely devastating. They had lost regular contact, but for Basquiat he was still a father figure. Basquiat went into a tailspin, ignoring potential buyers for his work, disconnecting the 'phone, asking friends to stay with him as though to protect him from himself. Only heroin seemed to calm him down. When he wasn't invited to Warhol's funeral in Pittsburgh, he was deeply hurt: it was a measure of how far Basquiat had fallen in status in the New York art world and amongst Warhol's entourage, people who had once been friends. He had to do with attending Warhol's memorial, with 2000 others, on April 1st in St Patrick's Cathedral. True to form he was late for the service. Basquiat now withdrew even further into drugs, 'chasing the dragon' with intensely powerful Tibetan heroin.

WHERE?
ANDY WARHOL'S MEMORIAL SERVICE,
ST PATRICK'S CATHEDRAL,
FIFTH AVENUE,
NEW YORK.

6

MISSISSIPPI

"He took me to the Mississippi. It symbolised a bond between us, because of the slaves..." Ouattara Watts

Basquiat had a show in Paris in early 1988, at the Galerie Yvon Lambert. At the opening he met a Francophone artist from near Abidjan, Côte d'Ivoire, called Ouattara Watts. Basquiat and Ouattara hit it off – they were like old friends, speaking French, touring art shows in Paris together. In Paris Basquiat also met musician Brian Kelly, suggesting that he was planning to quit painting to become a writer or musician, and possibly escaping NYC by going upstate or to Hawaii. It was clear that Basquiat was desperately looking for a new direction, one away from the caustic art crowd, critics and the dealers. He was also digging into his feeling of being an outsider and exploring his consciousness as a black man. That April he went with Ouattara to the jazz festival in New Orleans. They visited the Mississippi – a ritual acknowledgement of the slaves who had travelled down the river in search of liberty. Basquiat was trying to forge a new identity.

WHERE?
THE CRESCENT CITY CONNECTION
ACROSS THE MISSISSIPPI,
NEW ORLEANS IN THE DISTANCE.

7

THE LAST NY SHOW

"He looked really awful. He was talking about how everything was just fucked up and he hated his life." **Diego Cortez**

Basquiat's ever deeper descent into drugs now meant that no established dealer wanted to deal with him. Into the breach stepped Vrej Baghoomian, an Iranian expat who had helped his cousin, Tony Shafrazi, with his gallery. At a meeting at The Odeon he somehow managed to get Basquait to accept him as his agent. Baghoomian had a dilemma – he knew the reputed $400,000 a year he would pay Basquiat would probably go on drugs, but if he didn't give Basquiat the money he couldn't deal in his work. Baghoomian put up with the drug issues, becoming a surrogate father, trying to ensure that Basquiat didn't OD. He hired an assistant – Rick Prol – and Kelle Inman, a new girlfriend, moved into Basquiat's loft. He did produce some work, shown at the Cable Building in April 1988 – his last NYC show. Jennifer Goode showed up, but refused Basquiat's request that they get back together. One image featured the words 'Man Dies', a reference to Basquiat's self-destructive path, and a morbid premonition.

WHERE?
BASQUIAT AT HIS LAST NY SHOW,
CABLE BUILDING.
611 BROADWAY, SOHO,
MANHATTAN.

(8)

HAWAII

*"He started drinking in the morning,
he was drinking all day."* **Kelle Inman**

After the Cable Building show, with perhaps the realisation that he would
only get Jennifer Goode back if he came off heroin, Basquiat made
a desperate attempt to detox. He went to Hawaii on his own, to the
isolated promontory of Hana – accessible only by chopper or a winding,
single-track, perilous three hour drive. He called Inman back home,
sounding great – describing how he was playing music, fishing with the
locals, and how he was done with painting and was going to be a writer.
She joined him out there, but instead of heroin he was now drinking very
heavily, a way of killing the cold turkey. On the way back, he stopped
in L.A., behaving with weird good humour – he was off drugs, he said.
He asked to stay in a seedy hotel, away from any of the dealers at the
Chateau Marmont or L'Ermitage. He was drunk – mostly tequila – every
day. Back in New York he bumped into Haring, admitting to his habit (as
if it wasn't well known) for the first time, by saying he'd finally kicked it.

WHERE?
HANA COASTLINE,
HANA,
MAUI,
HAWAII.

9

GREAT JONES STREET

"I don't want to sit around here and watch you die." Kevin Bray, note to Basquiat

Basquiat started planning his clean future. He had a flight booked to Abidjan for August 7th, to go and paint with Ouattara, and to try a ritual cleansing to enforce his detox. But he was late getting back to NYC, so rescheduled for the 18th. Back in the loft he began using again – "just bingeing a little". An old friend of Steve Torton's was now dealing drugs daily to Basquiat, helping him to shoot up; they even discussed the danger that he might OD. But he was still optimistic, even going to see a house to buy in upstate New York, with Baghoomian and Inman. On the 11th August he was looking bad again but managed to go with Inman to a Bryan Ferry afterparty that night. He then wandered off, looking for Jennifer Goode. He didn't find her, but returned to the loft with a few friends. Completely spaced out, he crashed out upstairs – boiling hot as the aircon was broken. The next day Inman went to deliver a message to Basquiat. She found the most significant black artist of his generation lying lifeless on the floor, clear vomit dribbling from his mouth. Attempts to resuscitate failed. Basquiat, 27, was dead.

WHERE?
57 GREAT JONES STREET,
NOHO,
MANHATTAN.

BASQUIAT: 1988 – THE LAST YEAR

After the very unexpected death of Warhol in February 1987, Basquiat went into decline. He had broken up with his dealer Mary Boone, and no other dealer picked him up until Vrej Baghoomian agreed to a show. Basquiat now attempted a serious detox, bu travelling to Hana Hawaii. Travelling back to New York via L.A., he claimed to have kicked the habit. He planned a return to Abidjan for a ritual cleansing, but that wasn't to be. Basquiat ended his days in Andy Warhol's Jones Street Loft. He was 27.

KEY
- ● Travel and Show attended by artist
- ● Show not attended by artist
- ● Travel only
- ● Planned trip that didn't happen

❺ HANA, HAWAII
June
Basquiat travels alone to detox. Later joined by Inman Kelly.

❶ NEW YORK
January
First show in NYC for 18 months: one night at Baghoomian Gallery, the Cable Building.

❹ NEW YORK
April
Solo show at Baghoomian Gallery.

❻ LOS ANGELES
July
Basquiat claims he has kicked drug habit.

❼ NEW YORK
August 12th
Basquiat dies from an OD in his Great Jones Street loft.

❸ DÜSSELDORF
February
Solo show at Galerie Hans
Mayer

❷ PARIS
February
Solo show at Galerie Yvon
Lambert.

❽ ABIDJAN
August
Basquiat reschedules New
York–Abidjan flight from
7th August to 18th August.
Sadly he didn't make it.

AFTERLIFE

The moment he died, anyone with an interest in Basquiat realised
that his work would now shoot up in value. He hadn't written a will, so
everything that was his reverted to Gérard and Matilde, who was living
in a delapidated house in Bushwick, the poorest section of Brooklyn.
Gérard moved fast and Matilde agreed to have him represent her
interests in Basquiat's estate. He hired lawyer Michael Stout, who had
handled the estate of Salvador Dalí. The first step was to secure the
Great Jones Street loft and then the warehouses containing his work.
The loft was a mess and needed cleaning out, not least the hypodermic
syringes. Christie's began the careful months of work cataloguing
Basquiat's chaotic holdings, not just his own work, but Warhols,
Lichtensteins and Mapplethorpes. Then the usual legal wrangles
began with claimants to Basquiat works, Vrej Baghoomian and Kelle
Inman included. Given how the relationship between Basquiat and his
galleries was essentially a cash one, with barely any documentation,
this was inevitable. Gérard wanted nothing to do with anyone who
had represented Basquiat in the past, so he chose the uptown Robert
Miller Gallery to handle the estate. This was now estimated to be worth
up to $20 million. Baghoomian now sued the Robert Miller gallery,
Gérard Basquiat personally and the Basquiat estate, claiming he had
an "express understanding with the artist" that he should charge of
handling the estate. He sought $30 million in damages. He got a
temporary injunction, but no more.

Then Basquiat prices started climbing sharply at auction. There was a retrospective at the Whitney in 1992. Fake Basquiats started appearing on the market. In 1996 Julian Schnabel released *Basquiat,* a movie of Basquiat's life. Then things went quiet for a while. Interestingly, absurdly few institutions had bought Basquiats whilst he was alive, with MoMA even turning down a gift of a painting from the Schorrs. Saatchi never liked him. It was the collectors who amassed his considerable output and they have liked the work too much to sell. In general the work from 1981-1983 is the most prized. Scarcity, his iconic status as the most significant black artist ever, the raw, visceral genius of his work and the ultimately cool aesthetic of his images, have meant that prices have only accelerated. A wave of celebrity collectors have also recognised this, amongst them Elle Macpherson, John McEnroe, Leonardo DiCaprio, and Jay-Z and Beyonce.

When Matilde Basquiat died in 2009, her estate of Basquiat works was valued at $37 million. In 2013 Gérard, who had fiercely protected his son's legacy, not least by setting up an authentication committee to kick the fakes into touch, died. His estate was valued at $45 million. As collectors have died, so works have slowly come onto the market. But the great living collectors, the Schorrs included, are mostly holding onto their works.

Then, in 2017, one significant Basquiat work did appear on the market. Auctioned by Sotheby's that May, the painting, *Untitled*, achieved a remarkable $110.5 million. Jean-Michel Basquiat had finally earnt his crown: the sale anointed him as the most expensive American artist at auction, of all time.

WHERE'S BASQUIAT?

Very few art galleries around the world acquired Basquiats whilst he was alive: his work was too raw, too threatening, too cool for their rather Establishment view of the world. Now that his prices have reached stratospheric levels, they can no longer afford him. Astonishingly MoMA New York has no works: any it displays are on loan. The best way to see the power of his work is therefore at exhibitions. The two most significant to date have been Boom for Real in London in 2017, and the Basquiat show at the Louis Vuitton Foundation in Paris in 2018/19. The overwhelming number of works in both shows were loaned by private collectors. Between 2017 and 2019, the $110.5 million *Untitled* went on a world tour. It will be able to be viewed in Chiba, Japan.

LOS ANGELES
The Broad Modern Art Museum
13 works.

Museum of Contemporary Art
1 work.

BASQUIAT EXHIBITIONS:
2012
Arken, Denmark. Warhol and Basquiat. Arken Museum of Modern Art.
Miami. Masterpieces of the Berardo Collection. Gary Nader Art Center.
Avignon. Masterpieces of the Yvon Lambert Donation. Collection Lambert en Avignon.

2013
Zurich. Jean-Michel Basquiat. Galerie Bruno Bischofberger.
New York. Man Made: Jean-Michel Basquiat. Sotheby's S2.
Hong Kong. Jean-Michel Basquiat. Gagosian Gallery.
Seoul. Jean-Michel Basquiat.

2014
Vienna. Warhol/Basquiat, Kunstforum.

2015
Nashville.30 Americans. First Center for the Visual Arts
Little Rock, Arkansas.30 Americans. Arkansas Art Center
Toronto. Jean-Michel Basquiat: Now's the Time, Art Gallery of Ontario.
Bilbao. Jean-Michel Basquiat: Now's the Time, Guggenheim.

2016
Detroit. 30 Americans. Detroit Institute of Arts.
New York. Words Are All We Are. Nahmad Contemporary.

NEW YORK
Soho Contemporary Works
8 works.

Whitney Museum
1 work.

KEY
- Galleries with Basquiat holdings.
- Basquiat Exhibitions.
- Untitled World Tour.

BASEL
Fondation Beyeler
2 works.

BARCELONA
MACBA
1 work.

2017
Denver. Basquiat Before Basquiat.
London. Boom for Real, Barbican Art Gallery
Rome. Jean Michel Basquiat, Chiostro del Bramante.

2018
Frankfurt. Boom for Real, Schirn Kunsthalle
Paris. Basquiat, a Retrospective. Louis Vuitton Foundation

2019
New York. Jean-Michel Basquiat. The Brant Foundation.
New York. Basquiat's *Defacement*. Guggenheim.

UNTITLED WORLD TOUR

May 2017
Brooklyn Museum, New York.

March 2018
Seattle Art Museum

November 2018
Foundation Louis Vuitton, Paris.

January 2019
Chiba, Japan.

①

BASQUIAT: THE MOVIE

"Julian understands how to tell a story."
David Bowie

There was a time, early on, that Basquiat would have been thrilled to be in the same stable as Schnabel, who had his first solo show at Mary Boone in 1979. It is ironic that, having eclipsed Schnabel in terms of fame, and the two not having been close during his life, he should have been the subject of Schnabel's first feature film, in the process helping launch Schnabel's film career. The idea had come from Polish filmmaker, Lech Majewski. Schnabel bought out his research and collected an amazing ensemble cast, who worked for scale: David Bowie (as Warhol), Dennis Hopper (as Geldzahler), Gary Oldman and Willem Dafoe. Tom Waits and John Cale composed the soundtrack, for reduced fees. The film, which cost a modest $3.3million to make, received reasonable reviews, helping to develop the Basquiat myth. But for Jeffrey Wright, the newcomer who played Basquiat, Schnabel failed to capture the dangerous edge to Basquiat's nature, and scenes reflecting Basquiat's desire to escape to Hawaii featured surfing. Basquiat had no interest in surfing, not least because he couldn't swim.

WHAT?
BASQUIAT MOVIE RELEASE POSTER,
PREMIERED AT PARIS THEATER,
NEW YORK CITY.

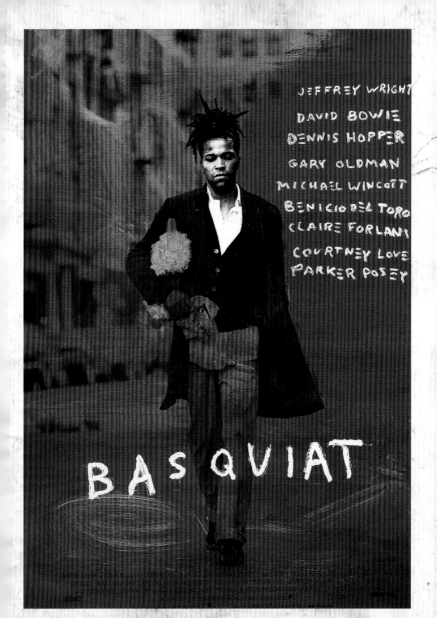

JEFFREY WRIGHT
DAVID BOWIE
DENNIS HOPPER
GARY OLDMAN
MICHAEL WINCOTT
BENICIO DEL TORO
CLAIRE FORLANI
COURTNEY LOVE
PARKER POSEY

BASQUIAT

②

BANKSY HOMAGE

"Major new show opens at the Barbican – a place that is normally very keen to clean any graffiti from its walls."
Banksy's Instagram

The first big exhibition in the UK of Basquiat's work, at London's Barbican Art Gallery, was a revelation. Over 100 works featured and the show illustrated how Basquiat worked across painting, drawing, objects, poetry, performance and music. One room recreated the room of his works featured in 1981's New York/ New Wave show. The show was a triumph. But the clincher was this brilliant homage by Banksy, inspired by Basquiat's 1982 *Boy and Dog in a Johnnyjump*. Not only is Banksy drawing a witty parallel – he too became the world's best known artist by starting on the street (although Banksy has avoided art world nightmares by very cleverly staying there) – but he is also capturing the crassness of the white bourgeois appropriation, through the gallery system, of black culture, and the inherent racism of the police: burning issues in London as well as NYC.

WHERE?
BARBICAN CENTRE,
THE CITY,
LONDON.

③

THE MOST EXPENSIVE AMERICAN ARTIST, EVER.

"He's now in the same league as Francis Bacon and Picasso."
Jeffrey Deitch, in *The Telegraph*

Yusaku Maezawa, a Japanese billionaire and founder of Japanese online fashion mall Zozotown, bid $110.5 million at Sotheby's New York on May 18th, 2017, for Basquiat's 1982 *Untitled* – an image of a skull. Basquiat, who painted the image when he was 21, was crowned the most expensive American artist ever at auction. He would have been amused that he pipped his icon and Pope of Pop Art, Andy Warhol (his *Silver Car Crash Double Disaster* made $105.4 million). *Untitled* had last sold in 1984 for $19,000 and had not been seen in public for over 30 years. Maezawa planned to make up for this by sending the picture on a short 'world tour'. When it comes to buying Basquiat, the billionaire has form: in 2016 he paid $57.3 million, then also a Basquiat auction record, for *Self Portrait*. Maezawa is planning to show the paintings in a museum he is planning for Chiba, Japan, his hometown.

WHERE?
YUSAKU MAEZAWA AT THE OPENING OF THE
BASQUIAT SHOW, FONDATION LOUIS VUITTON,
PARIS.

BASQUIAT RISING

$1
1978 Basquiat postcard, bought by Andy Warhol.

$200
1980 *Cadillac Moon*, bought by Debbie Harry

$3,500
1981 *Poison Oasis*, bought by Herb and Lenore Schorr

$10,000
1983 *Untitled* (painted 1983) bought by Herb and Lenore Schorr at Fun Gallery

$19,000
1984 *Untitled* (painted 1981) bought by Jerry and Emily Spiegel
(see last item on this list)

1987 BASQUIAT DIES

"There was a time in the 1990s when he was dismissed as a lightweight. Museums rejected him as a jumped-up wall-sprayer."
The Guardian

AND THEN:

$4.5 million
2004 *Untitled* (painted 1982), Sotheby's New York. Bought by Adam Lindemann.

$20.1 million
2012 *Untitled* (painted 1981), Sotheby's New York.

$23.7 million
2012 *Undiscovered genius of the Mississippi Delta* (painted 1983) Sotheby's New York.

$25.9 million
2012 *Untitled* (Yellow tar and feathers) (painted 1982) Sotheby's New York.

$26.4 million
2012 *Untitled* (painted 1981) Christie's New York.

$28.9 million
2013 *Untitled (diptych)* (painted 1982) Christie's New York.

$29.3 million
2013 *Untitled* (painted 1982) Christie's New York.

$48.8 million
2013 *Dustheads* (painted 1982) Christie's New York.

$34.8 million
2014 *Untitled* (painted 1981) Christie's New York.

$37.1 million
2015 *The Field Next to the Other Road* (painted 1981) Christie's New York.

$57.3 million
2016 *Untitled* (painted 1982), Christie's New York.
(This was the picture bought by Adam Lindemann in 2004).

$110.5 million
2017 *Untitled* (painted 1982), Sotheby's, New York.
(This was the picture bought by Jerry and Emily Spiegel in 1984 for $19,000. Sold by their daughter, Lise Spiegel Wilks).

WHERE WILL BASQUIAT GO NEXT?
WATCH THIS SPACE.....

CREDITS

Photo credits below are listed in section and page title order. Graffito wishes to thank all individuals and picture libraries who helped track down often elusive images.
In credits below, Alamy = Alamy Stock Photo.

A VERY BRIEF CHILDHOOD
Park Slope Alamy
Basquiat Senior Alamy
Flatbush Alamy
Gray's Anatomy Alamy
St Ann's Brooklyn Steve Minor
Puerto Rico Alamy
Washington Square Alamy
City-As-School Mme B. Cendrars
Birth of Samo Alamy

PERFECT TIMING
School of Visual Arts Alamy
The Mudd Club Alamy
East 12th St Alamy
WPA Restaurant Alamy
The Times Sq Show Alamy
New York Beat Alamy
New York/ New Wave Rex Features
Mudd Club Alamy

RUSH OF SUCCESS
Modena Alamy
Annina Nosei Alamy
West 23rd St Rex Features
Culebra Alamy
101 Crosby St Rex Features
Charlie 'Bird' Parker Alamy
Gagosian Rex Features
Chateau Marmont Alamy

BOOM BOOM BOOM
Bruno Bischofberger Rex Features
Girlfriends Rex Features
St Moritz Getty Images
The Whitney Alamy

WARHOL AT LAST
Fun Gallery Alamy
West 81st St Getty Images
Great Jones St Getty Images
Michael Stewart S.K. Gamin
Collaborations Alamy
Mary Boone Alamy
Area Getty Images

BOOM TO BUST
Palladium Rex Features
Les Bains Douches Getty Images
Shafrazi Gallery Getty Images
Abidjan Alamy
222 Bowery Rex Features
Warhol R.I.P. Getty Images
Mississippi Alamy
The Last NY Show Rex Features
Hawaii Cover Images
Great Jones St Getty Images

AFTERLIFE
Basquiat: **The Movie** Alamy
Banksy Homage Paul Mendoza
The Most Expensive American Artist, Ever Cover Images

This is a completely **unauthorised** publication. The contents, analysis and interpretations within express the views and opinions of Graffito Books Ltd **only**. All images in this book have been produced with the knowledge and prior consent of the picture libraries and photographers concerned.

Art Director:
Karen Wilks
Managing Editor:
Anthony Bland
Research Editor:
Serena Pethick

A note on the author.
Of Anglo-Spanish parentage, Ian Castello-Cortes grew up in South America and Cambridge, England. He is a publisher and writer with a particular interest in contemporary counter-cultures. Ian studied Modern History at Oxford University.

First published in the United States of America by Gingko Press, August 2019.
Published under license from Graffito Books.
Gingko Press, Inc.: 2332 Fourth Street, Suite E, Berkeley, CA 94710, USA.
Gingko Press Verlags GmbH: Schulterblatt 58, 20357 Hamburg, Germany.
ISBN: 978-3-94333-045-8